WOMEN
IN HISTORY

WOMEN AND EDUCATION

Anne Mountfield

Wayland

WOMEN
IN HISTORY

Women and the Arts
Women and Business
Women and Education
Women and the Family
Women and Literature
Women and Politics
Women and Science
Women and Sport
Women and War
Women and Work

Editor: Mike Hirst
Consultant: Professor Deirdre Beddoe, BA, PhD, Dip Ed, Reader in History at the Polytechnic of Wales
Series designer: Joyce Chester

Front cover: A class in a girls' school at the beginning of the twentieth century.
Back cover: Top left – A girl in a primary school class, 1970. Top right – Three women graduates at a graduation ceremony in the 1950s. Bottom left – Dr Barbara McClintock, a Nobel Prize-winning scientist, at her laboratory in the United States in 1947. Bottom right – A Victorian governess with one of her pupils.

First published in 1990 by
Wayland (Publishers) Limited
61 Western Road, Hove
East Sussex BN3 1JD, England

© Copyright 1990 Wayland (Publishers) Limited

British Library Cataloguing in Publication Data
Mountfield, Anne
  Women and education – (Women in history).
  1. Great Britain. Women. Education, history.
  I. Title. II Series.
376.941

ISBN 1 85210 647 6

Typeset by Kalligraphics Limited, Horley, Surrey
Printed in Italy by G. Canale C.S.p.A., Turin
Bound in the UK by MacLehose & Partners Limited, Portsmouth

Picture acknowledgements
Cheltenham Ladies' College 28 (both); ET Archive 8, 11, 13, 17; Mary Evans Picture Library *front cover*, *rear cover bottom right*, 7, 9, 10 (above), 12, 14, 15 (both), 16, 18, 20, 22 (below), 23, 24, 26, 30, 35 (both); Eye Ubiquitous 42 (above); Eileen Goodchild 39; Michael Holford 6; Hulton Picture Library *rear cover top right*; Ladybird Books 43; Billie Love 10 (below), 19 (below); Newnham College, Cambridge 32 (above), 33; Popperfoto 19 (above); Royal Holloway and Bedford New College 25; Society for the Promotion of Christian Knowledge 21, 22 (above); Syndication International 41; Topham Picture Library *rear cover bottom left*, 4 (both), 24 (below), 27, 31, 34, 36, 38 (both), 40, 42 (below), 44; Wayland Picture Library *rear cover top left*, 32 (below), 37.

Contents

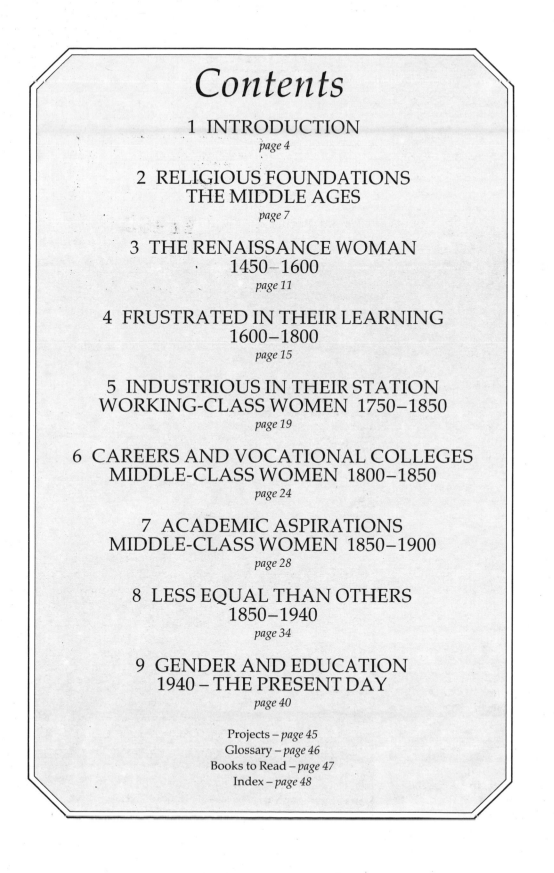

1

Introduction

Above When Elizabeth Butler-Sloss judges a case, the traditions of the legal profession require her to dress in a wig and gown like an eighteenth-century man.

Right Benazir Bhutto, who became prime minister of Pakistan in 1989, is a Muslim woman. She has been educated in Pakistan, England and the USA.

'It is not well done,' said Dr Samuel Johnson, the eighteenth-century writer and wit, about a woman preaching in public, 'but you are surprised to find it done at all.'

Today we are no longer surprised to see a few well-educated and confident women taking part in public life. A current affairs programme nowadays might include an interview with Diane Abbott MP, who is a Cambridge graduate, or Margaret Thatcher, a prime minister who has a chemistry degree and is a qualified barrister. The head of London University's Birkbeck College is a woman, Tessa Blackstone. Elizabeth Butler-Sloss is a High Court judge.

> **From the judge's seat to the legislator's chair . . . there is no post or form of toil for which it is not our intention to attempt to fit ourselves; and there is no closed door we do not intend to force open; and there is no fruit in the garden of knowledge it is not our determination to eat.**
> Olive Schreiner, in *Women and Labour*, 1911.

Until very recently, jobs like theirs were thought of as 'men's' work, an attitude reflected by their job titles: Tessa Blackstone is called the 'Master' of Birkbeck College; Elizabeth Butler-Sloss is referred to as a 'Lord Justice' and the prime minister is also the 'First Lord of the Treasury'. There has only ever been one female prime minister of the United Kingdom, and Dianne Abbott is the first black woman MP.

One of the reasons that women have not done jobs like these in the past is that they were not given the same educational opportunities as men. Throughout most of history, there have been fewer girls' schools than boys' schools, and until the late nineteenth century, women were not allowed to go to university at all.

Attitudes to the education of women have always depended on their role in society. For hundreds of years, women were considered to 'belong' first to their fathers and then to their husbands. They were not expected to want ambitious jobs which required an education, but to think that their chief duty was to care for their husbands and families. Hardly any women owned money or property in their own right and most men did not think it was worth spending money on educating women. A hundred and fifty years ago, a third of the men and nearly half of the women in England could not read or write. When they married or signed legal documents, poor people often marked their names with a cross. There were very few schools for anyone who could not afford to pay fees. But the proportion of illiterate women was always higher than that of men, because schooling for boys took priority in many families.

It is hard to know how women felt about their lack of education, or their low status in society, because so few were able to record their experiences. We can only guess a little about most women's lives from the things they made, or from what literate people recorded about them. We have no way of knowing how many women went through life with frustrated intellects and undiscovered talents.

Some women had the time and skill to write about their lives and about the relationship between women and men. But even if more women had written about these things, there was little chance of their work being published so that other women could read it. The views of early 'feminist' critics of society were not taken seriously by most men.

The women reformers who, over the centuries, campaigned for better schools for the poor, or for women's access to higher education might be amazed if they could see the opportunities open to women in Britain today. There are free state schools

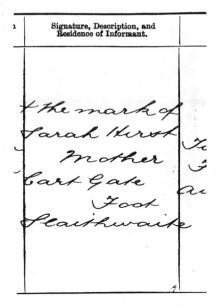

In 1890, Sarah Hirst could not sign her name when she registered her son's birth. Her children were the first generation to receive free state education.

❛ **In Nature we have as clear an understanding as Men, if we were bred in Schools to mature our brains.** Margaret, Duchess of Newcastle, 1655 ❜

hIC FECERVN: PRANDIVM: ET hIC EPISCOPVS:CIBV:ET POTV: BE NE DIC IT.

Although they may not all have been able to read and write, the women of the Norman court recorded the Norman invasion of England in 1066. The Bayeux tapestry shows their sense of design and their sense of humour.

for all children, which are bound by law to teach nothing to boys that is not on offer to girls. Universities and polytechnics admit both women and men. The educational provision for women is better than it has ever been.

But though educational opportunities have improved, the feminist campaigners of the past might be disappointed to see that many underlying assumptions have changed very little. Girls still do not get the same benefits out of the educational system as boys of similar background. Although girls do better than boys at the age of sixteen, they get fewer A level passes than boys; fewer women than men have degrees in mathematics, science and engineering; fewer women reach positions of influence at work. So why, in our relatively prosperous society, with laws that guarantee their right to the same educational opportunities as men, do women still underachieve?

Feminist educational reformers argue that it is because society still has 'sexist' assumptions which do not expect women to do the same things as men or to do them as well as men. Such hidden assumptions often lie beneath the treatment of women.

This book describes some of the ideas and events that have shaped attitudes to women and education. Though it deals with British history, many of the experiences it records find echoes today in the lives of women in other cultures and countries.

2

Religious Foundations

The Middle Ages

Many girls must have had teachers like the Nun Prioress in Chaucer's poem The Canterbury Tales. *She spoke French, but with a comical London accent, 'after the schole of Stratford-atte-Bowe'.*

Until the late Middle Ages, there were few schools of any kind and hardly any of them were for girls. Before the spread of the printing press in the fifteenth century, few people could afford books, and most people could not read. Most peasant girls, like their brothers, had all the educational training they needed in their homes, on the farm or by working in a big household.

Practical information was passed on, by word of mouth, from one woman to another. In this way, women pioneered the sciences of agriculture, cookery and food preservation. They developed the technologies of spinning and weaving, and the arts of making and decorating pottery and textiles. Women were the midwives who brought children into the world, the bard wives who sang stories and the old wives who helped the sick and the dying. These co-operative and practical forms of learning should be valued. But they could not, by themselves, answer the intellectual needs of all women, or equip women with the range of skills that would have freed them to compete for the same work as men, if they had chosen to do so.

In early history, almost all formal education was provided by the Church. The centres of learning were the religious foundations, and we know that some exceptional women flourished in these institutions. In 657, the wise and scholarly abbess Hilda founded the Yorkshire abbey of Whitby, where monks and nuns lived and studied alongside each other.

Throughout the Middle Ages, there were also a few girls' schools attached to nunneries. These schools trained girls to become nuns and also took in a few girls from rich or noble families as boarders. They taught their pupils to read and sing the Latin Psalter used in churches and to recite Latin prayers. Girl pupils might learn to make medicines for the poor or to embroider church garments and altar cloths for which nuns were famous.

Many abbesses and prioresses were important local figures, who must have set an example of female intellectual competence and managerial skill to their pupils. In the best of the nunnery

6

[The nunnery schools were] good Shee schooles, wherein the girls and maids of the neighborhood were taught to read and work; and sometimes a little Latine was taught them therein . . . Thomas Fuller, historian, writing in the reign of Charles II.

9

These nuns may have written and illustrated by hand the books they hold. What else is happening in this medieval picture?

schools, such as the one at Winchester, the girls might learn to read the Bible and speak in French, and in Latin, the most important language of medieval Europe.

However, standards of learning in the nunneries were generally lower than those of the monasteries, and even if girls were very bright, they could never rise to the main positions of power in the medieval Church, which were all held by men.

In the late Middle Ages, a new type of school began to appear in some towns. These were the 'grammar' schools, often founded by trade guilds. They charged fees to teach correct Latin and English grammar to local boys. There seem to have been some similar schools for girls, though we do not know much about them. The laws of the period, both in England and Scotland, refer to girls' schools, and to parents' rights to 'educate their sons and daughters' as they desire. There is also an early record of a schoolmistress, Maria Maresflete, who taught in a school in Boston, Lincolnshire, in 1404. Yet even if they were lucky enough to receive a grammar school education, girls were not allowed to study further at the universities of Oxford or Cambridge, where their brothers might go at the age of thirteen.

Although medieval women had only very limited access to books and schooling, they still often had to perform difficult jobs. The wives of medieval knights were expected to be competent managers in the home. They were responsible for hiring staff, ordering supplies and checking the household accounts. The women of the Paston family left a series of letters (1402–1509) that confirm their ability to run a household. Yet most of these letters were dictated to male secretaries. Only Agnes Paston's letters bear evidence of her own shaky efforts to write.

It was the custom for the children of better-off families to leave home at the age of seven or eight to be trained as waiting gentlewomen and pages. The purpose of this education was to teach them how to behave in polite society. Girls were taught a mixture of ladylike behaviour and elegant home management, which was a training for an early arranged marriage.

Some daughters of skilled tradespeople were also sent away from home, in their case to train as live-in apprentices. Their parents paid a mistress or master to clothe and feed the young apprentice, and teach her a craft or a trade, such as silk weaving or glove or hat making. These trades were organized by trade guilds that decided how things should be made, who could learn the trade and what wages should be paid. However, women did not find it easy to become full members of the guilds. Often they were admitted only if they were the widows of members.

Many goods were made in cottage industries, based in the family home. In private, women and girls might help their fathers and husbands with skilled 'men's' work. And at times of plague or warfare when 'manpower' was short (such as when the Black Death of 1348 wiped out nearly half of the population) women seem to have taken over from men, acting as wool merchants or guardians of prisons. But when the crisis subsided, women were no longer allowed access to the higher-paid, important jobs.

The lack of education for women during the Middle Ages was largely due to the attitudes which men held towards women generally. Women were either ridiculed or idealized. In

These women are combing out wool, spinning it into thread and weaving it on a loom. Can you tell which job was considered the most superior?

> **. . . these apprentices shall be bound by their indentures of apprenticeship to the husband and his wife, to learn the craft of the wife . . .** Ordinance of 1327

***Right** This image is of a lady sending her knight to the wars. He both protects and adores her.*

***Below** When a medieval woman argued too much, this 'scold's bridle' forced her to hold her tongue!*

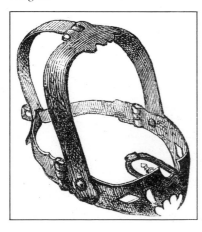

medieval literature, there are many comic portraits – all written by men – of women as scolds who nag their husbands, or as lazy gossips who cannot think logically. Yet some medieval writers also had a romantic image of women. Poets wrote about beautiful and virtuous, but delicate ladies, who needed the protection of a true knight.

The art and literature of the Middle Ages also make it clear how women were regarded by the Church. They appear either as chaste virgins, like the Virgin Mary, as holy mothers with young children, like Saint Anne, or alternatively as weak and wicked creatures, like Eve, who tempt men to sin.

Although these popular images of women were in many ways contradictory, they had one idea in common. Medieval men assumed that a woman's mind, like her body, was weaker and worked differently from that of a man. So women needed to be protected by men, or kept well away from the world of affairs. Above all, men believed that they were right to deny women access to the power of knowledge.

3

The Renaissance Woman

1450–1600

In the early years of Henry VIII's reign new ideas spread across Europe to England. The Italian Renaissance (or 'rebirth' of learning) produced a fresh interest in the arts and philosophy of ancient Greece and Rome. Explorers sailed from European ports to map out new worlds. From the new printing presses came demands to reform the Church.

Ideas about education also changed. In the sixteenth century, the emphasis shifted to the individual. The purpose of education became to develop the powers of mind and body. A 'Renaissance man' in the Tudor court studied languages, mathematics, astronomy, geography, history, law and religion. He learnt the arts of music, poetry and dance.

'
Go forward therefore with this your new and admirable skill, by which you thus climb up to the stars. Letter from Thomas More to his children, on their learning astronomy.
'

Sir Thomas More and his family. In later years More's daughter Margaret fearlessly defied the king who had executed her father.

Elizabeth I's signature, in her flowing italic script.

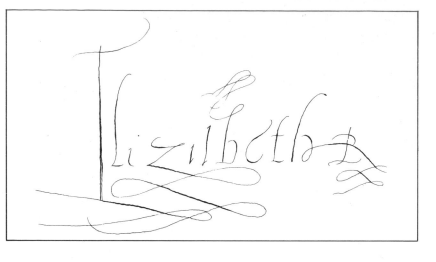

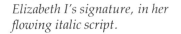

> *[Girls have] their own aptness to learn, which God would never have bestowed on them to remain idle or to be used to small purpose.* Robert Mulcaster, Tudor school master and the first Master of Merchant Taylor's School. **,**

> *The constitution of her mind is exempt from female weakness, and she is endued with a masculine power of application . . . French and Italian she speaks like English; Latin with fluency, propriety and judgement; she also spoke Greek with me, frequently willingly, and moderately well.* Roger Ascham on Queen Elizabeth I aged sixteen. **,**

The women of the noble and royal families proved that they too could reach a high standard of learning if they were given the chance. Sir Thomas More's daughters were so highly educated that his home was jokingly referred to as 'Plato's Academy'. Margaret, the eldest, was famed for her knowledge of languages and her ability to translate them from one to the other. Together with her sisters, she staged a disputation, a kind of debate, in front of the king.

But even a thoughtful man like Thomas More still believed that a woman's place was in the home. He was eager to give his daughters a full opportunity to extend their intellects. But he thought the purpose of a woman's education was to make her a 'more effective wife and mother'.

Catherine of Aragon, Henry VIII's first wife, came from Spain, where women were allowed to study at the universities. Catherine was anxious for her daughter, Princess Mary, to be taught by a Spanish tutor, Juan Ludovico Vives. The strict *Plan of Studies for Girls* which he prepared for the princess combined intensive learning with sermons on modesty of dress and censorship of her reading. Though Mary Tudor's education was narrow in outlook, it was broad in content; she studied not only languages but also science and mathematics.

Mary Tudor's half-sister Elizabeth was luckier. Her governess, Katherine Ashley, was congratulated by Roger Ascham, author of *The Scholemaster*, on the princess's excellent academic progress. Ascham, who later became the princess's tutor, believed in gentle methods of encouragement. Elizabeth became fluent in many languages and could translate from Latin to Greek. She also wrote accomplished poetry in her confident and stylish handwriting.

The English princesses are early examples of what today would be called female role models. Because they were admired for their learning, other girls were encouraged to follow their example. For a brief time it was considered fashionable for a woman to show evidence of her learning.

Yet even Queen Elizabeth I felt it necessary to explain to men that she was not like other women. In a famous rallying speech to her troops at Tilbury, she declared, 'I know I have the body of a weak and feeble woman, but I have the heart and stomach of a King, and a King of England too.' She was not the last successful role model to boost her own reputation by pulling down other women.

What impression of the young Queen Elizabeth I do you think the artist of this picture intended to convey?

Bathsua Makin (?–1673)

Bathsua Makin was, like many women reformers, educated at home by a clergyman father. In the Renaissance style, he taught his children sciences and mathematics, as well as ancient and modern languages. Bathsua was drawn to the sciences and also became interested in education. She was influenced by a Dutch educational writer, Anna Schurmann, who asked of women's inferiority: 'Is it God's law – or man's?'

Bathsua's brother Thomas was a courtier of Charles I, and in 1641 Bathsua herself was appointed to teach the royal children. She seems to have been given complete freedom to choose their curriculum. Under Bathsua's tuition the young princess Elizabeth learnt especially quickly and soon became 'proficient' in mathematics and many different languages.

Bathsua later took charge of a school for gentlewomen in Putney and in 1673 she published an *Essay to Revive the Antient Education of Gentlewomen*.

In this essay, Bathsua Makin described the decline in educational standards that she had seen in her lifetime. She herself retained the Renaissance ideal of a full education. But she claimed that, during the seventeenth century, standards of education for gentlewomen in England had declined. Girls were, she said, perfectly capable of learning and they deserved better. She was not amused by the old joke that, 'one tongue is enough for a woman'. She thought that women should learn foreign languages, not just as an 'accomplishment' but in order to study foreign ideas.

Bathsua Makin planned to open her own school, which would teach the usual subjects studied by young ladies: religion, dancing, music and basic reading, writing and counting. But to these subjects she added a series of choices: courses in Latin, French, natural history, astronomy, geography, Hebrew, Italian, Spanish, philosophy, art and domestic science. Hers was the first girls' school curriculum to give equal value to sciences and arts.

Forma nihil si Pulchra perit; sed pectoris alma
Divini species, non moritura viget.
W. M. sculpsit

The writing around this engraving of Bathsua Makin's portrait celebrates her knowledge of three different ancient languages: Latin, Greek and Hebrew.

4

Frustrated in their Learning

1600–1800

The Elizabethan fashion for learning, the decline of which Bath-sua Makin regretted, had always been restricted to noble women; and throughout the seventeenth and eighteenth centuries, there continued to be little educational provision for the vast majority of women. There were a few schools for the rich, such as the Ladies' Hall, Deptford (1617), but they were mostly finishing schools, with little to offer an intelligent girl.

One exception were the Quaker schools. The Society of Friends was a religious group which aimed to be a community of equals. It set up excellent boarding schools where girls were encouraged to express an opinion. But when Quaker women preached or spoke in public, most people made fun of their

Above *Mrs Elizabeth Montagu. She and her bluestocking friends gave each other intellectual and emotional support. Dr Johnson dismissed her writings on Shakespeare without reading them.*

> *Let not your girl learn Latin . . . for the pride of taking sermon notes hath made multitudes of women most unfortunate . . .* Ralph Verney to his god-daughter, Nancy Denton.

> *To make women learned and foxes tame had the same effect: to make them more cunning.* James VI of Scotland and I of England.

Left *How are the men reacting to this Quaker woman preaching?*

earnest manner and, despite their modest dress, thought the women's behaviour unseemly.

Women who dared to challenge the authority of men met strong resistance. One such woman was Newcastle-born Mary Astell (1668–1731). In her *Serious Proposal to the Ladies* which was published in 1694, Mary Astell suggested that a college should be set up where women could have time to discover the 'independent pleasure' of study. A rich lady agreed to back this proposal with a donation of £10,000. But plans were halted when an Anglican bishop claimed that this 'monastery for women' might be a plot to bring back Catholic convents!

Women needed intellectual support from each other. Yet in eighteenth-century England there were few places where intelligent women could meet to discuss ideas. However, one well known group of intellectual women began to gather in the London and Bath homes of the wealthy Mrs Elizabeth Montagu.

The atmosphere of Mrs Montagu's salon was literary and informal. One guest, Benjamin Stillingfleet, used to come unconventionally dressed in woollen blue stockings (instead of the more 'correct' black silk hose worn for evenings). As a result, both the male and female members of this witty and intelligent circle became known as the 'Blue Stockings'.

In later years this label became a term of ridicule applied only to women. The bluestocking woman might have brains but she was also portrayed as boring and dowdy. Clever women were sneered at as being unattractive to men. This scorn was (and still remains) an effective way for men to discourage unwanted female competition.

Late in the eighteenth century, many writers and thinkers were influenced by new ideas about the rights and equality of

The revolutionary women of the French Revolution frightened people in eighteenth-century England.

Many wealthy women spent hours every day in dressing elaborately. This eighteenth-century painting, by an Italian artist, shows a rich woman at her toilet.

all men. In America and France, revolutionary wars overthrew the old governments and introduced greater political freedom. Some people feared these new ideas were dangerous to the stability of society. But the woman writer Mary Wollstonecraft (1759–97) rejected them as not revolutionary enough. It was all very well, she argued, to talk of freeing the colonies or the peasants. But women, the largest oppressed group in society, still had no rights, including the right to equality in education.

Mary Wollstonecraft had run a school herself and knew that, given the opportunity, girls could be just as intelligent as men. She believed in coeducation, discussion methods, observing the interests of the child and offering girls advice about careers. In her *Vindication of the Rights of Women* she said that girls were damaged by an education that controlled their freedom and was not based on their needs.

Many of Mary Wollstonecraft's ideas are widely accepted today, but in the eighteenth century they were considered to be outlandish. Like many other women reformers, she was ridiculed by her male critics. During her lifetime, most intelligent women remained 'frustrated in their learning'.

Catherine Macauley (1731–91)

Catherine Macauley was a bluestocking historian and a radical political thinker whose views were not popular in her day. She was privately educated at home and wrote an eight-volume history of England, and political pamphlets which supported the revolutions in America and France.

Catherine was a mother who developed ideas about education by seeing her own children grow up. In 1790, she wrote her *Letters on Education with Observations on Religious and Metaphysical Subjects*. This work was one of the clearest, most original and earliest arguments for anti-sexist education.

In her *Letters on Education . . .*, Catherine challenged the idea that certain forms of flirtatious, spiteful or ignorant behaviour

adopted by women were inborn. Moreover, though herself striking in dress, she insisted that women should not feel compelled to dress in ways that caused them discomfort, just in order to make themselves attractive to men. Nor should they, 'lisp . . . totter . . . and counterfeit more weakness and sickness than they really have, in order to attract the attentions of a male.' Girls should be free to study the same sports and subjects as boys, she wrote, but boys too should be free to learn how to sew a button instead of being forced to conform with the masculine expectation that they would prefer hunting.

Catherine was an important figure in her day. She gave George III her uncompromising views about his controversial taxation of the American colonies, and Patrice Wright, a 'Yankee' woman who had a waxworks in Pall Mall, made a model of her. After the American Revolution, in which the colonies gained their independence from Britain, she stayed as a guest in the home of George Washington, the first president of the United States. Yet in England her views were always considered too radical for general acceptance.

'

Confine not the education of your daughters to what is regarded as the ornamental parts, nor deny the graces to your sons. Catherine Macauley, *Letters on Education.*

,

Mary Wollstonecraft wrote of Catherine Macauley, 'I will not call hers a masculine understanding because her profound thinking was proof that women can acquire judgement.'

5

Industrious in their Station
Working-class Women 1750–1850

By 1800, many well-to-do women were, like Catherine Macauley and Mary Wollstonecraft, insisting on women's right to a proper education. Yet most poor people, and especially poor girls, could still not even read or write. There were no government funds for schools and few families could afford private education. Many girls were sent out to work at the age of eight, or sometimes earlier, because their parents needed the money.

In society at large, great changes were under way. The Industrial Revolution had begun, and the new machinery and large factories had a dramatic effect on people's lives. In earlier centuries, mothers had often worked alongside their husbands as they laboured in cottage industries or in the fields. Their children had played nearby. During the Industrial Revolution, the

Above *Elizabeth Fry realized that poverty led to crime and that a proper education could help to prevent it.*

Below *During the Industrial Revolution, many women had to do low-paid work in the new factories. The overseers were usually men.*

This is a 'dame' school where children were minded for a small fee while their parents worked. What are these girls learning that the boys are not?

'

In by far the greatest number of these schools there were only two or three books among the whole number of scholars. In others there was not one; and the children depended for their instruction on the chance of some one of them bringing a book, or a part of one, from home. Report on the conditions in Dame schools in Lancashire in the 1830s.

'

workplace moved from the home to the factory and many more people lived in the squalid, crowded new towns. Women went to work in the factories, where it was difficult for them to look after their children.

Many wealthy people believed that the high rates of crime and drunkenness in the industrial slums could be blamed on the absence of women from the home. Working mothers, it was said, were failing in their traditional duty to provide the moral education and home comforts that would keep their husbands and children sober and honest. Women were held to be responsible for the good or bad behaviour of their families.

To improve the behaviour of the poor, middle-class people began to take an interest in charity schools. Many new charity schools for poor girls or poor boys were founded, often using money left in the wills of rich people, or the gifts of the well-to-do. The first charity school for girls had been the Red Maids School in Bristol (1634). It took its name from the warm red cloaks and hoods in which its pupils were dressed. Some schools, like Thomas Coram's Foundling Hospital in London, took in abandoned babies and orphans. These schools provided the children with a home until they were old enough to go out to work . All charity school pupils were taught to be grateful to their benefactors and were told that they should become honest labourers and servants. But poor girls learnt that they had a doubly inferior position in society. As women, it would be their duty to put their own needs after both the needs of their families and the demands of their employers.

During the eighteenth century, more middle-class women reformers, such as Hannah More, Elizabeth Fry and Mary Carpenter, became interested in the plight of the poor and of criminals. Educating the poor was usually considered to be worthwhile charity work, though even these women were sometimes criticized for what they did.

1817 the Quaker reformer Elizabeth Fry set up a school in Newgate prison for the children of the female prisoners. She was publicly accused of neglecting her own children in order to do this work. There was a double standard in society's attitude towards women. It was held that middle-class women and girls tired easily and needed to rest both their minds and bodies if they were to stay healthy. Few people suggested that working-class women tired easily. The comforts of too many people depended on their labours.

> *As soon as the Boys can Read completely well . . . teach them to Write a fair legible Hand, with the grounds of Arithmetic, to fit them for Services or Apprenticeships. Note the Girls learn to read etc. and generally to knit their stockings and Gloves; to Mark their Cloaths: and several learn to Write, and some to Spin their Cloaths.* SPCK instructions to teachers in charity schools.

(32)

Numb. III.

An ACCOUNT of the RATES of Cloathing
Poor Children belonging to CHARITY-SCHOOLS.

The Charge of Cloathing a GIRL.

	l.	s.	d.
3 Yards and half of blue long Ells, about yard wide, at 18d. p. Yard, makes a Gown and Petticoat	00	05	03
Making thereof, Strings, Body-lining, and other Materials,	00	01	00
A Coif and Band of fine Ghenting	00	01	00
A Shift	00	01	06
A White, Blue, or Checquer'd Apron	00	01	00
A pair of Leather Bodice and Stomacher	00	02	06
1 Pair of Woollen Stockings	00	00	09
1 Pair of Shoes	00	01	10
A Pair of Pattens	00	00	08
1 Pair of Buckles	00	00	01
1 Pair of Knit or Wash Leather Gloves	00	00	07
The Total	00	16	02

N. B. The different Stature of Children is allowed for here; and 50 Children, between the Ages of 7 and 12, (one with another) may be cloathed at these Rates.
The Particulars abovementioned may be had at Mr. R. Parker's, in Queen's-Court at St. Katharines by the Tower.

A page from an SPCK report, showing how much it cost to clothe a charity-school child.

A

SELECTION

FROM

MRS. TRIMMER'S

INSTRUCTIVE TALES.

The Unkind Daughter,
The Dutiful Daughter and Grand-daughter,
The Complaining Husbands,
The Over neat Wife,
The Desponding Couple,
The Notable Daughter,
The Jealous Wife,
The Drunken Husband,
The Wrangling Couple.

London:

PRINTED FOR F. C. AND J. RIVINGTON,
Booksellers to the Society for Promoting Christian Knowledge,
NO. 62, ST. PAUL'S CHURCH-YARD;
By Law and Gilbert, St. John's-Square, Clerkenwell.

1815.

Above *The first page of one of Sarah Trimmer's instructive books. What impression of family life do the titles of her stories give?*

For most poor people, the only opportunity for education was provided by the Church. Sunday Schools were set up and quickly grew in popularity. They taught children on their one day free from work in the factories, mills and coal mines. Women such as Sarah Trimmer (1741–1810), who had strong Christian principles, became active in the Sunday School movement. The schools taught reading and Bible study. Sarah Trimmer also thought that training for skilled work was important. In 1786 she set up an industrial sewing school, where poor girls could learn a trade.

Church organizations also increased the number of day schools for the poor. The Society for the Promotion of Christian Knowledge (SPCK) had run some schools since the early seventeenth century. In 1811 a new National Society for the Promotion of Education of the Poor took over the running of the Church of England schools from the SPCK. Non-conformist religious groups, such as the Methodists and Baptists, also ran schools. Both were open to girls as well as boys.

Yet the curriculum in these schools was limited. Girls and boys learned to read their ABC and simple sentences such as 'God is Love'. But they were not taught to write. Although wealthy people wanted to teach the poor to be honest and hard-working, there were also many fears that educating the poor would make them ambitious and rebellious, and forgetful of their place in society. So in schools for the poor, girls were taught to pray, 'Make me industrious after my station.'

Right *The amateur teachers in this 'Ragged School' look noticeably warmer and better dressed than the poor girls who are learning to read.*

Hannah More (1745–1833)

Hannah More was educated first by her father and, later, by her elder sisters who ran a boarding school. After an unhappy engagement, she vowed never to marry and became influenced by Evangelical Christianity. She was also a friend of the reformer William Wilberforce, who became famous for his campaign to abolish the slave trade.

In 1789, Hannah and her sister Martha visited Cheddar, in Somerset. The children of the poverty-stricken miners in the area were wild and ragged. The two More sisters set up Methodist Sunday Schools in Cheddar and other parts of the district. In these schools, the poor were taught to read the Bible and to know their Catechism. The girls were taught to spin.

The French Revolution of 1789 had made many people afraid of a similar revolution in Britain. Hannah More did not want to teach poor people to write because she thought reading was enough for them. She was also afraid that revolutionaries might use bloodthirsty 'broadsheets' – the only cheap reading matter available for the poor – to stir up trouble. She set out to imitate the popularity of these cheap story and news sheets, which were printed on only one side. Her *Cheap Repository Tracts* contained moral stories which were designed to encourage honesty. They were an enormous success and sold in millions.

Hannah More was equally conservative in her views about women's roles. In her *Strictures on the Modern System of Education* (1799) she called for changes in women's education. Yet she did not want women to be so 'puffed up with the conceit of talents' that they neglected their household duties.

Hannah More's ambitions seem limited today. But in her own time, many people thought she was endangering the stability of society, and wasting money, by giving even a basic education to the poor.

> *I allow of no writing for the poor. My object is not to make fanatics but to train up the lower classes in habits of industry and piety.*
> Hannah More.

As a young woman, Hannah More was a member of the famous Blue Stocking Society. In 1786, the year this portrait was made, she published a collection of poems called Bas Bleu.

THE
ENGLISH WOMAN'S JOURNAL.

PUBLISHED MONTHLY.

Vol. III.   June 1, 1859.   No. 16.

XXXVL—THE DETAILS OF WOMAN'S WORK IN
SANITARY REFORM.

Above *One of the first editions of* the English Woman's Journal.

6

Careers and Vocational Colleges

Middle-class Women 1800–1850

For centuries, a woman's financial support came first from her father and later from her husband. Upper and middle-class girls were especially dependent upon men; unlike poor girls who could at least earn a small wage, the women in better off families were not expected to work. It was important for them to make good marriages. Their limited education was therefore designed to help them attract a suitable husband.

In Georgian England most young ladies were taught to read and write at home, either by their mother or by a governess. They might, like the novelist Jane Austen (who did not marry), attend a private day school or a boarding school for a short time. But these schools taught little beyond reading and writing, French conversation and how to behave politely.

Middle-class families often had several visits a week from private tutors. Girls were taught to sketch and paint water-colours; they learned to dance and sing and to play a musical

Mamma NOW GO AND SAY GOOD-NIGHT TO YOUR GOVERNESS, LIKE A GOOD LITTLE GIRL, AND GIVE HER A KISS.
Little Puss I'LL SAY GOOD-NIGHT, BUT I WON'T GIVE HER A KISS.
Mamma THAT'S NAUGHTY. WHY DON'T YOU GIVE HER A KISS?
Little Puss BECAUSE SHE SLAPS PEOPLE'S FACES WHEN THEY TRY TO KISS HER.
Mamma NOW, DON'T TALK NONSENSE AND DO AS YOU'RE TOLD.
Little Puss WELL MUMMY, IF YOU DON'T BELIEVE ME – *ASK PAPA!*
The life of a governess could be difficult – in many ways.

instrument, usually the piano. They read novels aloud, made pictures from shells, pressed flowers, embroidered and visited the poor. Most girls' lives were an empty round of what the exasperated Hannah More dismissed as merely 'a phrenzy of accomplishments'.

The Industrial Revolution created a new, prosperous middle class of traders and shopkeepers, engineers and accountants. In an effort to make their daughters 'ladylike', they copied this upper-class style of education.

The education that produced a lady of leisure did not fit her to earn her own living. Unmarried women or widows who were not provided for in the will of their father or husband were dependent on the charity of their male relatives. If it was not forthcoming, the only 'respectable' career for a middle-class woman was teaching.

Some of the more adventurous single women went to teach overseas, as missionaries, or as teachers and governesses in the British colonies. But most middle-class women who needed to work stayed in Britain. They taught in private schools or as governesses. If a governess failed to satisfy her employers, she lost both her job and her home. In 1841, the Governesses' Benevolent Institution was founded to help governesses with short-term money problems. One of its first actions was to set up an employment register.

It soon became clear that many British governesses were themselves very poorly educated. Parents often preferred to employ a governess from France or Switzerland. This was partly because French and Swiss women were good at teaching French conversation. But it was also because they had been trained in their own countries and given a teaching diploma.

In England the only teacher training colleges in the 1840s were run by the church societies, to train elementary school teachers. In 1836, the Home and Colonial Infant School Society began offering twenty-week courses for teachers. In 1841, the National Society founded what was later to be called St Mark's College in Battersea. By 1845 there were thirteen training colleges, six of them for women.

The Governesses' Benevolent Institution began to set exams that were open to governesses and women teachers. The results confirmed how ill-educated many of these women were. To make amends, Queen's College (1848) was opened in London, to provide 'compensatory education' for girls who wanted to teach. The following year, Bedford College was set up by Nonconformists. Unlike Queen's College, and unusually for its day, Bedford was to be managed by women as well as men.

Be good sweet maid and let who will be clever
Do noble things not dream them all day long.
And so make life, death and that vast forever
One grand sweet song.
Charles Kingsley

Bedford College was founded as a teacher training college. It later became a full college of the University of London.

What 'accomplishments' is this Victorian girl displaying? Notice her tiny waist; girls were taught to keep themselves thin.

> *. . . how society fritters away the intellect of those committed to her charge.* Florence Nightingale in her privately printed book, *Cassandra*.

Some girls who came to the colleges entered a four-year course at the age of twelve. There were evening classes for older girls who were already teaching during the day. The two colleges were really like secondary schools and Adult Education Institutes. They offered girls, for the first time, the chance of being taught an academic subject by a university graduate. But as yet all the graduate teachers were men.

To some determined women it did not seem fair that teaching was the only acceptable career for a middle-class girl. In 1812 Miranda Barry had managed to train as a surgeon at St Thomas's Hospital – but only by pretending to be a man! Florence Nightingale came from a wealthy family that was anxious for her to marry and settle down. She refused, insisting that she wanted to train in Germany as a nurse. This idea was shocking at a time when nurses were thought to be dirty and drunken. But when Florence reached the age of thirty, and was still unmarried, her family reluctantly gave in.

Florence Nightingale went on to find fame as the 'lady with the lamp' who nursed wounded soldiers in the Crimean War and who campaigned for better military hospitals. By the end of the war in 1857, she was a national heroine and the grateful British public presented her with money. She used it to set up the Nightingale School of Nursing. Nursing then became, with teaching, one of the twin vocations considered suitable for a woman. They also became two of the lowest-paid professions.

A cousin of Florence Nightingale, Barbara Leigh Smith, was a leading member of the Langham Place Ladies' Circle. This group took its name from the street in which its women members rented meeting rooms. Their aim was to improve the opportunities open to women of all social classes. The 'Ladies of Langham Place' set up a Society for the Promotion of the Employment of Women. It encouraged fresh areas of employment for lower-middle-class women, as bookkeepers and cashiers in shops. In 1859 the Langham Place group created a voice for themselves by publishing the first feminist magazine, the *English Woman's Journal*. It called for women to be free to choose their own careers, to control their own financial affairs, and to be given the vote. As a first step, the *English Woman's Journal* called for an improvement in girls' academic education, and for women's entry to the universities.

Florence Nightingale in old age, with some of her students. The student nurses of St Thomas's Hospital, where her school began, are still known as 'Nightingales'.

Above Dorothea Beale had a strong influence on the development of girls' schools.

7

Academic Aspirations

Middle-class Women 1850–1900

Two of the most famous pioneers of secondary education for women were Dorothea Beale and Frances Mary Buss. Both women attended Queen's College and both became famous headmistresses. Dorothea's first headship was of the College itself, when she was still only twenty-three. Neither she nor Frances Buss married – women teachers were expected to remain single and if they had married, they would have lost their jobs.

Both Miss Beale and Miss Buss believed that women needed an academic education, and were capable of making good use of it. But their ideas about education differed in ways that were to shape the two different philosophies of secondary schooling for girls.

> *Miss Buss and Miss Beale*
> *Cupid's dart do not feel,*
> *They leave that to us,*
> *Poor Beale and poor Buss!*
> Popular Rhyme.

Right Cheltenham Ladies' College, of which Dorothea Beale was an early headmistress.

Frances Buss believed that there was no significant difference between boys and girls that need affect their education. (Nor did she think there was a significant difference between a clever girl from an upper-class home, and one from a lower-class family, other than their access to learning.) Girls must work hard, she said, in order to catch up with the historic advantages boys had long enjoyed. They must be prepared to compete with boys in order to prove their abilities, and this competition must be on equal terms if women wanted to be taken seriously.

Dorothea Beale also agreed that girls must be allowed access to academic education. But she was more sympathetic to the view that women had special qualities of caring which must be preserved. She did not believe that the competitive approach, with its aggressive team games and exam lists in order of merit, was the best one. These were not the best methods of teaching, she thought, even if they were the traditional methods of boys' schools. The education she offered her girls should widen their intellectual horizons, but should also bear in mind their future needs as people in society.

In 1858, Dorothea Beale became the headmistress of Cheltenham Ladies' College, a boarding school for the daughters of 'noblemen and gentlemen'. The Cheltenham parents were conservative in their views about such matters as the teaching of mathematics. One father wrote to the new headmistress: 'My dear lady, if the girls were going to be bankers it would be very well to teach them arithmetic as you do, but really there is no need . . .' Since they were destined only for marriage, what was the point?

Like many early headmistresses, Dorothea Beale had to struggle against the prevailing idea that girls would damage their reproductive organs if they played too much sport, that they needed more rest than boys and that, because their brains were smaller, they could not tackle too much learning at once. She achieved the academic curriculum she wanted, which was a blend of academic work and considering what one could do for others. Exams took place, but competition was not encouraged. By wishing to develop their minds, women ought not to acquire the worst characteristics of men.

While Dorothea Beale was working in Cheltenham, Frances Buss also put her ideas into practice, at the North London Collegiate School for Ladies (later called North London Collegiate School for Girls), which opened in 1850.

Because it was a day school, not a boarding school, the North London Collegiate could offer parents a secondary education for their daughters at a moderate price. Though the teaching

Women are supposed to be very calm generally; but women feel just as men feel; they need exercise for their faculties, and a field for their efforts as much as their brothers do . . . Charlotte Bronte, in *Jane Eyre.*

The mistresses at Sheffield Girls' High School in 1890.

was uneven and inexperienced, the school was a great success. By the end of the first year, the number of pupils had risen from 35 to 115. At first, the school was open only in the mornings, so that girls could rest or pay calls in the afternoon, but Frances Buss soon persuaded parents that their daughters could cope with a full day's schooling.

In 1871, Frances Buss opened Camden Lower School, where the fees were kept deliberately low so that clever girls from lower-middle-class families could attend. She took a great interest in the new government elementary schools and encouraged her girls to undertake social service and to be aware of conditions among poorer classes.

In 1868 there was a government report, from the Taunton Commission, into the conditions in boys' grammar schools. The commissioners decided they would also examine the girls' secondary schools. In answer to pleas for more girls' schools, they came up with an idea that stirred deep controversy but was at last accepted. The Endowed Schools Act of 1869 allowed some of the money that had been endowed to old grammar schools by their founders to be transferred for the building of new grammar schools for girls.

In 1872 Maria Grey set up the Girls' Public Day School Trust, which administered the affairs of a group of day schools for girls. It aimed to give girls the same opportunities that were available in the boys' public schools. Though the girls' grammar schools often lacked science equipment and qualified science teachers, they pioneered academic secondary education for

6

I am repeatedly told that cooking, the government of servants . . . the right management of the purse, and the power to economize all the resources of the household are of more importance to a girl than learning. All this is confessedly true. But then these things are not taught in the schools. Taunton Commission Inspector, 1869.

9

those girls whose parents could pay fees. The GPDST schools included North London Collegiate, and were usually run on the competitive lines approved of by Frances Buss.

The number of girls' boarding schools also increased at this time, though they varied greatly. Some were strongly academic; some were latter-day versions of the finishing schools of the eighteenth century, and some were, like Cheltenham College, a blend.

At the same time as some women struggled to expand secondary education for girls, others were fighting to gain access for women to the universities. During the 1860s, there were many suggestions for a general reform of the old universities and proposals for the foundation of new ones. Yet there was still resistance to women students. Even London University, which,

> *The equal right of all women to the education recognized as the best for human beings; the equal right of girls to a share in the existing educational endowments of the country; and . . . the registration of teachers, with such other measures as may raise teaching to a profession as honourable for women as for men.*
> Principles for female education, as suggested in a lecture by Maria Grey, founder of the GPDST.

Some people mocked the idea of the new educated woman – and her companion, the new man. What does the artist think the new woman is escaping from?

in its 1836 Charter claimed to offer education to, 'all classes and denominations . . . without any distinctions whatsoever', was slow to accept women. It set separate exams for them in 1866 and did not give them full equality with men until 1878.

One of the strongest advocates of university education for women was Emily Davies. In 1872, she became the first mistress of Girton College for women in Cambridge, and she fought long and hard for her students to be allowed to sit university exams alongside men from other colleges. Yet Cambridge in particular held out for many years against a full acceptance of women. Even after they had passed the same exams as men, women were not allowed to attend a proper graduation ceremony; and the university did not grant women full degree status until 1948.

Some men claimed that women should not be given a university education because they would not be able to study difficult subjects as well as men. But by the end of the century, these claims had been proved wrong. In 1890, a woman, Philippa Fawcett, gained the top marks in the Cambridge Mathematics Examination. Frances Buss celebrated the occasion by giving a special speech to her school. She told her girls that in 1865 she had appeared before the Taunton Commission and sceptical men had asked her whether she thought women could learn mathematics. Though they had pushed her into admitting that none of her own pupils was sufficiently advanced to learn maths at the time, she had insisted, 'Yes, I am sure they can and they will.' Twenty-five years later, she proudly announced, 'Today, those gentlemen have their answer!'

Right *At Newnham College, Cambridge, there were celebrations when one of the women students beat all the men in a mathematics examination.*

Anne Jemima Clough (1820–92)

Anne Jemima Clough was a teacher who first worked in schools for poor children in Liverpool and Southwark. In 1867 she joined the reformer Josephine Butler in setting up the North of England Council for Promoting the Higher Education of Women and helped to organize some of the first university extension lecture tours. These courses, given by visiting lecturers, were very popular with both women and men, especially as there were no universities except Durham in the north of England at that time.

With Anne Clough as its Secretary, the North of England Council began to press for special women's examinations at university level. It came into direct conflict with Emily Davies, who passionately believed that women should tackle the same exams as men or lose credibility. However, Anne Clough's scheme met with some success and in 1869 Cambridge University set a higher local examination for women.

In 1871, Anne Clough became the head of Merton Hall, Cambridge, where women attended the lectures that would prepare them for the new examination. In 1879, the Hall became established as Newnham College, with lecturers in residence, and Anne Clough as its first Principal.

For several years the Newnham women continued to sit separate exams, and Anne Clough and Emily Davies never fully reconciled their differences. Emily Davies believed that education involved a power struggle for equality with men. In her opinion, Anne Clough's efforts to support and protect her students made her back away from the necessary confrontation.

However, Anne Clough had a wider experience of the pressures on women's lives. Above all, she wanted to fit women's education to their current needs. Although she believed in change, Anne Clough was also prepared to compromise and move more slowly than Emily Davies. The two women represented different approaches towards reform which still exist today.

Anne Jemima Clough and Newnham College of which she was the first principal.

8

Less Equal than Others

1850–1940

In the late 1860s, British politicians at last began to consider introducing compulsory elementary education for everyone. British industries were threatened by foreign competitors in the race for new products and markets, and industrialists blamed their failures on a shortage of skilled workers. Moreover, although the vote had been given to some working-class men in 1867, many of them could not read their ballot papers. The country needed properly educated workers, but there were too few schools, cramped buildings, under-trained teachers and too little equipment.

In 1870 and 1880, new Acts of Parliament first increased the provision of elementary education and then made it compulsory, although parents were still asked to pay a small fee. In 1891 elementary education became free for children between the ages of five and twelve. For the first time, no matter how poor their parents, or how insistent that the boys' needs should come first, all girls had the right to a free elementary education until they reached the age of twelve.

Although the Acts of Parliament gave girls an equal right to education by law, in practice they did not get it. Attendance by girls was lower than that by boys. If a child in the family was sick, or a mother had a new baby, a schoolgirl would often be expected to help out at home. Teachers and school managers accepted that this was necessary. A boy was a 'truant' but a girl was an 'absentee'. Fewer efforts were made to ensure that girls attended school regularly.

The schools that were built and funded by the government were known as 'Board schools', because they were managed by locally elected school boards. Many of the new schools were built for both girls and boys as an economy, to make the building costs lower. But they were 'mixed', not coeducational, schools. Usually there were separate classrooms for girls and boys, or rows of boys on one side of the room and rows of girls on the other. School playgrounds were kept separate, to protect the supposedly weaker girls from the rough play of the boys.

In elementary schools, only the girls were expected to learn cookery.

Left *At Board Schools, children learnt to write on slates which could be cleaned and reused.*

Each year, inspectors visited the school to test the pupils' progress. Any who failed to meet the standard had to repeat a year. The old story of different and lesser treatment for girls was repeated. Needlework was compulsory for the girls. They did sewing and housecraft while the boys learned carpentry in the workshops. In some schools needlework for girls was time-tabled against arithmetic for boys. The inspectors expected the girls to reach a lower standard than the boys in arithmetical calculations. It all helped to make people, not least the girls themselves, think that 'girls can't do maths'.

The curriculum was, in any case, unimaginative and uninspiring. The harassed teachers issued instructions to their large classes like drill sergeants: 'Lift slate! Clean slate!' Pupils read paragraphs of facts aloud, recited spellings and multiplication tables, and copied down dictated sentences in careful handwriting. Their mathematics was seldom more than mental arithmetic, with sums involving only money, weights and measures. If geography or history were taught at all, it was mostly in the form of set questions and answers: 'What are the five main rivers of England?' 'When was the battle of Hastings fought?'

Below *Girls at the turn of the century, being trained for work as laundry maids.*

The schools saw their task as vocational training for the work that the children were likely to do in the future. Boys would need to earn a 'family' wage; girls were likely to marry and have a large family. So boys must be given the chance to become apprentices or clerks, while girls need only aspire to domestic service, laundry work or a job in the low-paid clothing industry. Working-class girls thus suffered not only from the class disadvantage of being offered a limited and vocation-based curriculum, but also from the assumption that the earning capacity of a man should take precedence over that of a woman.

'Swedish gymnastics' were introduced to British girls' schools at the end of the nineteenth century. In the 1920s, the 'gymslips' being worn in this picture were seen as a way to give girls greater freedom of movement.

The differences in what boys and girls were taught continued long into the twentieth century. In 1922, the Hadow Report examined the differences in the curriculum appropriate to the 'needs of boys and girls'. Many of the teachers interviewed thought that girls were less capable of prolonged mental effort than boys and believed that there should still be two separate curricula for the different sexes.

By the 1890s, many elementary schools were teaching a few of their brighter pupils more than the limited and unimaginative set syllabus. The children who stayed on beyond the age of twelve went into classes called Standard VII and Standard VIII. This was, in effect, a form of secondary education designed for working-class children.

The 1868 Taunton Commission had also required a girls' secondary grammar school to be set up in every town with a population of more than 4,000 people. The 1902 Education Act gave local authorities the responsibility for elementary and secondary schools in their area, and allowed them to build extra classrooms for the older elementary school pupils. Some local authorities provided for older children by building new secondary central or technical schools.

The technical schools were often single sex and the curriculum for girls always emphasized shop work, typing and office skills. Many parents were opposed to their daughters going on to secondary education when they could be out earning, or helping in the home. Even the grammar school scholarship, which was a proud achievement in a boy, was frequently seen as just a waste of money for a girl. The scholarship covered the cost of education, but the parents had to pay for uniform, books and equipment. 'What's the point?' said many families. 'She'll only go and get married.'

> *The attempts recently made to economize by teaching boys and girls together, abolish the headmistress by putting a head master over boys and girls alike . . . is only a revival under a new guise of the old idea that girls are not entitled to the same consideration as boys.*
> Alice Zimmer, 1898.

A cartoon from Punch *in 1916. The idea of careers for women was still being mocked.*

Above These girls' grandparents must have been shocked to see them play competitive games like men.

Below 'Red' Ellen Wilkinson combined concern for women's education with concern for more general social issues.

By the early decades of the twentieth century, a small number of girls from wealthy families, or highly able scholarship girls, were given an academic education. But the number of women in grammar schools and at university was always far smaller than that of men; and the career opportunities open to women at the end of their education were far more limited.

Middle-class feminists now faced a problem that was in clearer focus than it had been in the eighteenth century. What should they concentrate on – the inequality between women and men, or that between rich and poor? In the early twentieth century, some women were chiefly interested in 'The Cause' of female suffrage and women's academic education; others decided that the welfare of the working class as a whole must take precedence in their lives. A few women have looked for ways to combine the cause of socialism with that of 'Women's Rights'. Clementina Black worked for the Women's Industrial Council and 'Red' Ellen Wilkinson, a Labour MP, became the first woman minister of education. Yet, in spite of their efforts, working-class women continued to be the group in society with least access to educational opportunities.

Eileen Goodchild (1920–   )

Eileen Goodchild was born in 1920, above the London fire station where her father was a firefighter. She went to elementary school, and when she was eleven she sat a scholarship examination. It was, she says, an exam that 'channelled brighter or luckier working-class children into the central schools which groomed them for high-grade work in business and industry.' She passed, and went on to the Oratory School for Girls. Her school courses were designed primarily as a business training, and she studied economics, shorthand and typing.

Eileen was a good scholar. But during the economic depression of the 1930s, there was a lot of pressure on children to leave school and try to get a job as soon as they reached the standard school-leaving age of fourteen – especially the girls, who were easier to employ, because they were paid less than boys. So, she says, 'I was fortunate that my father allowed me to stay on at school until I was sixteen.'

Eileen went straight from school to work as a clerical officer in the civil service. During the war, she was called into engineering work, and later she married, had a family and did not return to full-time work until her youngest daughter was sixteen.

On her retirement at sixty, Eileen decided she would at last, 'fulfil what I hadn't been able to do when I was young', and study at university. She became a student at the Open University, and in 1989 she finally received the degree that she had wanted for so long.

The Open University was set up in 1964 as the 'University of the Air'. Eileen listened to lectures that came to her on television or

Eileen Goodchild in her gown, after the ceremony at which she was awarded a degree by the Open University.

radio. She sent work by post for a tutor to mark. In the summer, she also attended summer schools where the students and tutors can meet.

Eileen Goodchild's university education has enabled her to start a new career, lecturing in the sociology of design at Glasgow School of Art. Her experience shows that education can be lifelong. There are now many ways in which women who missed out at school can study, at their own pace and without qualifications, and even, if they wish to do so, inside their own homes.

' ━━━━━━━━━━━━━━━━━━━━━

[The Open University is for] all those, who, for any reasons, have been precluded from achieving their aim through an existing institution of higher education.

━━━━━━━━━━━━━━━━━━━━━ **'**

Dora Black in 1920. With her husband, the philosopher Bertrand Russell, she ran a coeducational school which taught equality between the sexes. She soon found that her famous husband believed more in the theory than in the practice.

9

Gender and Education

1940 – The Present Day

In 1944, a new Education Act aimed to create 'one nation' out of the class divisions that existed in Britain. Three kinds of secondary school education were made available: grammar schools, technical schools, and the new secondary modern schools. In theory the places were to be allocated on the basis of the intelligence tests of the eleven-plus exam, which claimed to show 'aptitude and ability' for the three kinds of learning. In practice more children from the middle classes went to grammar schools and the secondary modern schools were filled with working-class children.

Nevertheless, the new system did have the effect of creating an educational ladder for working-class pupils. Entry to the grammar school could lead some children to higher education and to social and career opportunities that had previously been beyond their reach.

Some girls benefited from this system. Books and equipment were free, so girls who passed the eleven-plus were seldom actually held back from attending the grammar schools, as they once had been. But more girls than boys tended to leave grammar school as soon as they legally could, and before they had taken the exams at sixteen. Because most of them stopped full-time work when they married, they did not generally achieve the same career successes as the grammar-school boys.

From the late 1950s on, the separate types of school began to be replaced by comprehensive schools seeking to provide education suited to the 'aptitude and ability' of individual children within a single school. The arguments raged about which system was better for academic standards, for the advancement of working-class children and for supplying a skilled work-force. Very few people ever thought to ask which system was best for girls.

Many people still took it for granted that there were innate differences of outlook and ability between girls and boys. The Crowther Report of 1959, which looked at the provision for fifteen to eighteen-year-olds recommended courses for less able

It feels so sad to be a woman! Men seem to have so much more choice as to what they are intended for. Vera Brittain, *Chronicle of Youth* (Gollancz, 1981.)

When the first calculating machines were introduced into classrooms in the 1960s, the newspaper caption read: 'These schoolgirls have a friend named Tom. He takes the muddle out of maths for the girls in the picture.'

girls in personal appearance, fashion and human relationships. The explanation had a fine disregard for scientific evidence, stating baldly that 'the incentive for girls to equip themselves for marriage and home-making is genetic.' As for boys, 'at this stage their thoughts turn more often to a career and only secondly to marriage and the family.'

Girls were underachieving and no one seemed to notice. However, the pattern of underachievement was not straightforward, especially below the age of sixteen. In 1970, girls of eleven were doing better than the boys in intelligence tests, reading and arithmetic. By fifteen, the girls had dropped slightly behind – or perhaps the boys had just caught up. Fewer girls than boys were entered by the schools for O level subjects, but in the exams they sat, the girls on average scored more highly than the boys. More or less the same numbers of girls and boys left school at sixteen. The most significant figure confirmed the observation that, for whatever reason, girls seemed to prefer 'verbal' subjects like English, Modern Languages and History, while the boys chose 'spatial' and numerical subjects like sciences, technology and maths. In 1970, out of all the pupils taking maths, 40 per cent were girls and 60 per cent boys.

After the age of sixteen, it was easier to see how the girls were falling behind. More girls left school after one year in the sixth form. More boys than girls obtained A level passes and far more boys than girls passed in science and maths. Though more girls went on to further or higher education, the girls

Right Like the working-class girls of Victorian England, black girls today are doubly disadvantaged. They face prejudices about their gender and their colour. The book Motherland *records one girl immigrant being told that, 'as she was from Trinidad, she should be especially good so that she could be an example to others'.*

6

Currently, education and schools play a significant role in constructing male supremacy and in perpetuating male dominance and control. Dale Spender.

9

Below Frances Murray, the Royal Navy's first female Air Engineer Officer. She was the only woman among four hundred students at the Naval Engineering College in 1981.

went into lower status institutions and trained for lower status jobs. The 1975 Sex Discrimination Act had made all courses and options open to girls and boys alike. The puzzle was that so often the girls themselves seemed to choose not to do certain things: they chose not to study sciences and maths, though these led to better-paid jobs than secretarial work; they chose not to go to university and not to compete with men for top positions in business and industry.

Over the past twenty years, feminists have begun to ask why fewer women make the most of educational opportunities than men. In 1980, the Australian feminist and teacher Dale Spender helped to edit a book of essays called *Learning to Lose*. This book drew attention to a number of ways in which sexism affects girls in school. It examined the hidden assumptions about the ways women should behave and the jobs they should do. These assumptions still govern the way many people think, and not least the way women see themselves. Influenced by feminists like Dale Spender, many teachers have begun to look more closely at what goes on in their classrooms and inside their pupils' homes.

The social pressures put upon girls to behave in certain ways are described by feminists and educationalists as 'gender' issues. (The term gender is used because it is a more neutral word than 'sex'.) The word gender is used to show us that the unequal treatment of women is not an inevitable result of their biological differences from men. Gender roles are not 'natural';

they are the result of social assumptions about the appropriate roles for each sex.

Today many teachers and parents are becoming aware of the ways in which attitudes are passed on from one generation to the next. They are now less likely to ask for a 'big strong boy' to help them move the furniture, or for a 'nice tidy girl' to help them clean out a cupboard. Publishers know that it is no longer

I am helping Daddy to mend the fence.

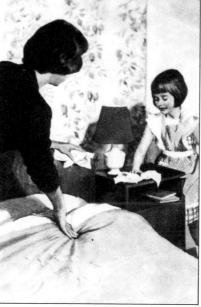

I am helping Mummy to dust.

What do these pictures tell you about the social assumptions of their day? They are taken from a school book produced in the 1950s.

acceptable for Mummy to spend her life baking cakes in the kitchen while Daddy goes out fishing or mends the car. There are fewer places where the boys come first on the register lists, or have the football playground all to themselves.

Attention is turning to more subtle forms of sexism: do teachers give as much time and attention to the girls as they do to boys? Why are boys so dominant in the classroom? Why do they often have first use of the technical equipment? What is the effect of being taught by someone of the opposite sex? Is a single-sex school better for girls? And are boys equally oppressed by the tough image that they are expected to present?

The next chapter in the history of women and education has still to be written. It is not yet clear what kinds of change will take place in the next hundred years. But there will be some change, if only because in the labour force of the future, society will need as many highly qualified women as possible. It may be that once again conditions will change while underlying attitudes remain unaltered. Yet many feminists intend their use of the word gender to give hope. If society has created gender assumptions, then it is the duty of members of society to challenge the damaging aspects of these attitudes which place limitations on the lives and happiness of both women and men.

How would you educate a daughter or a son?

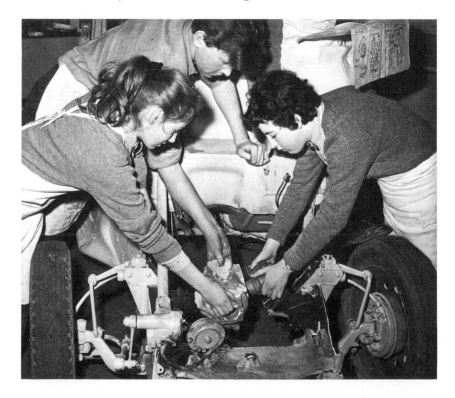

In 1963, seventeen pupils in a Corby grammar school helped to build a car with a two-cylinder steam engine. Twelve of the pupils were girls – which contradicts the findings of the Crowther Report.

Projects

Oral History

Ask your mother, grandmother, women teachers and any other women who are willing to help you, if you can interview them about the ways girls were treated in their school-days. Try to include some women who were not born in this country. Use a tape recorder if possible.

Find Out:

Who chose the kind of school they attended?
Was it a single-sex or a coeducational school?
If coeducational, how was the classroom organized?
Did the girls feel intimidated by the boys?
What subjects did they study and what choices did they have?
How many women teachers did they have, teaching which subjects?
How much career guidance did they have?
How did they, and the adults in their lives, regard their contacts with boys?
How were they disciplined?
How much were they expected to help at home?
Did their families value their education?

What differences do they notice in the education of girls today?

You may like to use your researches to produce a book, a radio documentary or a play about women's education in this century.

Primary Evidence

Ask if you can see the early records of your school, or of one in the area that admits girls. What do they reveal about the way girls were treated? How many women were on the staff in the early days, teaching which subjects? How many are there today?

In Your Local Area

Draw up a list of the girls' or coeducational secondary schools in your area.
What kind of schools are they?
Have they always been like that? (eg. comprehensive, coeducational.)
When were they built?
How many of them have women heads?
Make a similar survey of primary schools.

What women's work can you see in a local museum?
Has the museum any records of local school work by girls in the past?

Glossary

Astronomy The study of the stars and planets.

Catechism A book which contains the teachings of the Church in question and answer form for children to learn.

Coeducation Educating boys and girls together.

Cottage industry An industry in which things are made by people working in their own homes. Before the Industrial Revolution, many goods were manufactured in cottage industries.

Curriculum A course or programme of study.

Denomination A group or sect of Protestants, such as Anglicans, Baptists, Methodists, etc.

Endow To provide with or bequeath to a person or institution a permanent income.

Feminist A person who advocates equal rights for women.

Finishing school A school at which a girl is taught social graces and accomplishments, rather than academic subjects.

Gender The state of being male or female. Feminists use the word gender when they refer to social stereotypes of how men and women should behave.

Illiterate Unable to read or write.

Industrial Revolution The period of British history, from about 1750–1850, when many new industries and ways of manufacturing goods developed.

Literate Able to read and write.

Non conformist A Protestant who does not conform to the teaching of the Anglican Church. In nineteenth-century Britain, there was great rivalry between Anglicans and Nonconformists.

Religious foundation A place where a group of people live together, following the rules and doctrines of a religion.

Renaissance The period in Europe, from about 1450–1600, when people rediscovered the learning of the Greeks and Romans, and began to question the beliefs of the Middle Ages.

Role model A person whose behaviour or way of life is an example followed by many other people.

Salon A meeting at which friends discussed art, literature and politics.

Sexist Someone or something which discriminates against a person on the basis of their sex.

Trade guild An organization of people who all practise the same trade. In the Middle Ages, trade guilds were very powerful, and regulated the way in which many things were made, and the wages of the workers.

Vocation An occupation or career. Usually one into which a person puts much time and effort.

Books to Read

Factual books for older readers

Busher, Hugh *Education since 1800* (Macmillan Education, 1986)

Deem, Rosemary *Women and Schooling* (Routledge & Kegan Paul, 1978)

Equal Opportunities Commission *Do You Provide Equal Opportunities?* (Equal Opportunities Commission, 1979)

Fletcher, Sheila *Feminists and Bureaucrats (Girls' Education In The Nineteenth Century)* (Cambridge University Press, 1980)

Fraser, Antonia *The Weaker Vessel* (Methuen, 1984)

Mitchell, Juliet and Oakley, Ann *The Rights and Wrongs of Women* (Penguin, 1976)

Spender, Dale and Sarah, Elizabeth *Learning To Lose* (The Women's Press, 1980)

Turner, Barry *Equality For Some* (Ward Lock Education, 1974)

Weiner, Gaby (ed.) *Just A Bunch of Girls* (Oxford University Press, 1985)

Woolf, Virginia *Three Guineas* (Hogarth Press, 1986)

Woolf, Virginia *A Room of One's Own* (Granada, 1977)

Factual books for younger readers

Allen, Eleanor *Young in The Twenties* (A & C Black, 1988)

Hodgson, Joyce *Women in Society* (Macmillan, 1989)

MacDonald, Fiona *Women History Makers – A Chance to Learn* (Macdonald, 1988)

Fiction

Austen, Jane *Emma*
Austen, Jane *Mansfield Park*
Austen, Jane *Northanger Abbey*
Brontë, Charlotte *Jane Eyre*
Brontë, Charlotte *Villette*
Dickens, Charles *Hard Times*
Eliot, George *Middlemarch*
Fielding, Sarah *The Governess* (Pandora, 1987)

For fiction books that are set in girls' schools between 1839 and 1975, see the very full list at the back of:

Cadogan, Mary and Craig, Patricia *You're a Brick, Angela! (Girls' Fiction 1839–1975)* (Victor Gollancz, 1976)